This book belongs to:

_____

Cast of Characters

POLIDORI   CLAIRE   BYRON

SHELLEY   MARY   THE MONSTER

For the kids who love to daydream and imagine. — L.B.

For Tara Walker — J.S.

This paperback edition first published in Great Britain in 2019 by Andersen Press Ltd.
First published in Great Britain in 2018 by Andersen Press Ltd.,
20 Vauxhall Bridge Road, London SW1V 2SA.

Text copyright © 2018 by Linda Bailey
Illustrations copyright © 2018 by Júlia Sardà
This edition published by arrangement with Tundra Books, a division of
Penguin Random House Canada Limited.

Printed and bound in China

1   3   5   7   9   10   8   6   4   2

British Library Cataloguing in Publication data available.

ISBN 978 1 78344 763 3

I am very grateful for the help of Dr. Maggie Kilgour, Molson Professor of English Language and
Literature, McGill University, Montreal, who kindly reviewed this book and provided invaluable
feedback and thoughtful insights. Any errors, omissions or inaccuracies are my own.
Huge thanks to the incomparable Tara Walker for bringing her editorial excellence to this book —
and many more thanks to the wonderful team at Tundra Books, especially Margot Blankier,
Liz Kribs, John Martz and Peter Phillips.
— Linda Bailey

MARY
AND
FRANKENSTEIN

WRITTEN BY
Linda Bailey

ILLUSTRATED BY
Júlia Sardà

HOW DOES
A STORY BEGIN?

Sometimes it begins
with a dream.

Here is Mary. She's a dreamer. The kind of girl who wanders alone, who stares at clouds, who imagines things that never were. Mary has a name for her daydreams. She calls them 'castles in the air'.

Mary loves stories too. She tries to write the kind that she reads. But the stories she sees in daydreams are the most thrilling of all.

And where does she go to read and dream? She goes to a graveyard and sits at her mother's grave.

Mary's mother was a great thinker. She wrote books to say that women should have the same rights as men. She died when Mary was only eleven days old.

Can you miss someone you've never known?

Mary does.

Mary's father is also a thinker. He taught Mary to read by tracing the letters on her mother's gravestone. Mary loves her father, but he can be strict and stiff. And when he's upset with her, he grows cold and silent... until she cries.

Before very long, he marries again.
Mary doesn't like the new wife.
The new wife doesn't like Mary, either.

Famous people visit their London home. Philosophers, artists, scientists, writers.

One night at a party, a writer named Samuel Taylor Coleridge recites a strange, eerie poem — *The Rime of the Ancient Mariner*. Mary *loves* such poems. But she has been sent to bed.

She wants so badly to listen that she hides behind a sofa. She and her stepsister shiver with fear at the spine-tingling tale of a ship full of ghosts.

For the rest of her life, Mary will remember this night. And she will *never* forget that poem.

Mary is angry and unhappy at home, and she shows it. By the time she's fourteen, she has become a Big Problem. Her father sends her away to live with a family of strangers in Scotland.

The family is kind. Mary likes them. As she wanders the barren hills, she can let her imagination roam free. But at sixteen, when she returns to her family, she is still a Big Problem.

And what does she do next?

She becomes an even Bigger Problem. She runs away
with a brilliant young poet. Her stepsister, Claire, goes
along too. The poet's name is Percy Bysshe Shelley.
Like Mary, he's a dreamer.

Mary's family are horrified!

With very little money, the young people travel in Europe by horse and donkey, and on foot. They also take a boat down the Rhine River. One day they tie up the boat near a ruined castle. It's called Castle Frankenstein.

Such an interesting name!

Does it stick in Mary's mind?

But it's on their next trip together, eighteen months later, that things get *really* interesting. On this trip, Mary, Shelley and Claire travel to Switzerland, where they make friends with a famous poet.

Lord Byron is the most famous poet in the world.
(He's also famous for being handsome.) He is staying in a
beautiful house beside Lake Geneva. On breezy spring
days, they can go sailing!

But summer brings mysterious storms. Dark clouds rumble and churn.

One evening comes the wildest storm of all. Lightning rips the sky. Thunder booms! Rain lashes the house beside the lake.

Inside, five people sit huddled beside the fire. Two young women. Two poets. A medical doctor.

The doctor is a friend of Lord Byron. His name is John Polidori, and he loves to write.

What can such people do on a night like this?

Only one thing.

It's a night made for...

Ghost stories!

Byron opens a book of ghoulish stories called *Fantasmagoriana*.
In the flickering firelight, he begins to read.

As the others listen, their mouths go dry. Their scalps
prickle. Their hair stands up. They can almost *see* the ghostly
apparitions dancing on the walls.

Such is the power of a scary story on a stormy night.

At the end of the evening, Byron
suggests a contest. "We will each write
a ghost story," he says.

Whose will be best?

Remember now, who is in this room.
Two brilliant poets, one of them famous.
A doctor. Two very young women.
Mary is only eighteen.

And what happens next? Well, according to Mary...

Shelley and Byron begin their stories right away, and so does Polidori.

"Do you have an idea?" they ask Mary.

"No," she says.

Every day, they ask her again. "Have you thought of a story?"

"No," she says.

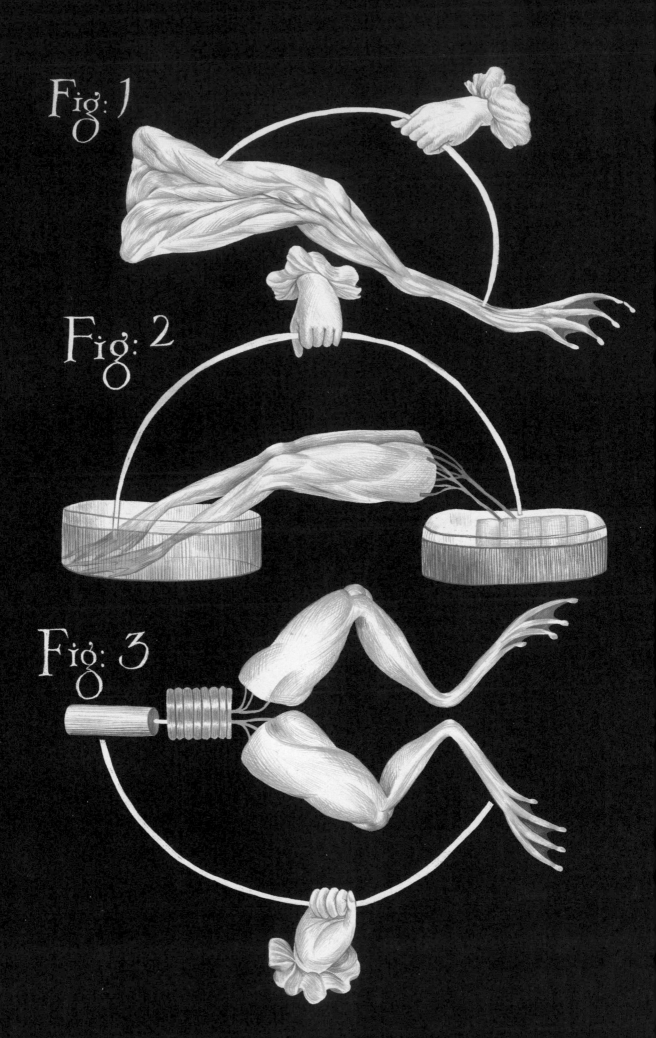

Shelley and Byron get bored. They stop writing stories. They
start to plan a sailing tour around the lake instead. And they
talk one evening — as they've been talking all summer —
about new discoveries in science. Exciting experiments!
Electricity can make the muscles of a dead frog twitch. Could it
bring a dead creature to life?

The idea is both thrilling and frightening.

Mary listens. Later, she goes to bed. But she can't fall asleep. Instead, in that strange, lost time between wake and sleep, she has a kind of day-dream. She sees a hideous monster, made of dead body parts, stretched out — and coming to life! The scientist who made the monster is so scared by what he's done, he runs away.

Mary opens her eyes, frightened. She tries to forget what she imagined. She tries to think up a ghost story instead.

And then, with a sudden jolt of excitement, she understands. She has already *found* her ghost story! The monster coming to life. *That* is the story she will write. Finally, she has her idea.

The next morning, she sits down and writes these words: "It was on a dreary night of November..."

The writing of *Frankenstein* has begun.

It takes nine more months of daydreaming and writing for Mary to finish her story. Two publishers say no to publishing it. A third publisher finally agrees to make it into a book.

The first people who read *Frankenstein* are sure it was written by Percy Shelley. They don't believe young Mary could have done it! How could a girl like her come up with such a story?

But maybe *you* know.

She wrote a scary story about a scientist named Victor Frankenstein who brought a dead creature to life and then became frightened at what he had done.

Scary story. Frankenstein. Dead creature. Scientific change. Where did such ideas come from? And how did they come together?

In a writer's imagination.

In a dream.

Writers dream stories, awake and asleep.

MARY WOLLSTONECRAFT
GODWIN
Author of
A Vindication
of the Rights of Woman
Born 27th April 1759
Died 10th September 1797

Over two hundred years have passed since that night beside the lake. And everywhere around the world, people know Mary's book. It has become a legend! It may be the greatest scary story of all time.

And now you know how it started...

It began with a girl named Mary. She liked to daydream and imagine.

And she grew up to write *Frankenstein*.

Author's Note

Mary Shelley (1797–1851) wrote her extraordinary novel *Frankenstein; or, The Modern Prometheus* when she was only eighteen years old. The book that she wrote was astonishing. But no less remarkable is the story of how she wrote it.

Mary told this story in her author's introduction in 1831, thirteen years after the book was first published. When I reread this introduction a few years back, I wondered whether it might make a picture book — and as I began to explore the many fine adult biographies of Mary Shelley that have appeared in recent years, I was quickly enthralled. Mary's life, by both accident and choice, was rich with drama. It was filled with the kind of powerful themes that are written again and again in fiction. I discovered, in fact, that there were actually many stories within the story of Mary's life and creativity.

One is the story of a motherless child. Mary's mother, Mary Wollstonecraft, was an early hero of feminism and the illustrious author of *A Vindication of the Rights of Woman*. She died eleven days after Mary's birth. Mary's father, philosopher William Godwin, remarried after Wollstonecraft's death, but young Mary's love and loyalty were always reserved for the mother she had never known.

Sadly, Mary's life was also a story of people who died too young. Three of her four children with poet Percy Bysshe Shelley (whom she married in late 1816) died tragically early in childhood. Also among those who died too soon were Mary's fellow participants in that night of ghost stories. Percy drowned in a sailing accident aged twenty-nine.

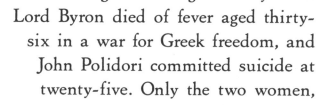

Lord Byron died of fever aged thirty-six in a war for Greek freedom, and John Polidori committed suicide at twenty-five. Only the two women,

Mary and her sister Claire, survived into middle age.

Mary's story is also very much a love story — filled with passion, rebellion, sacrifice and loss. From beginning to end, her relationship with Percy was tumultuous and often painful. As writers, Mary and Percy inspired one another, and Percy acted as both editor and agent for Mary's manuscript.

To readers of *Frankenstein*, of course, the most gripping story about Mary is one of literary creativity — the tale of the inspirational evening of ghost stories, culminating in Lord Byron's challenge and Mary's later vision of a scientist staring down at a creature he had formed from human body parts and was now bringing to life. It took Mary nine months of hard, disciplined work to complete a first draft.

Frankenstein was published in 1818. After a modest start, it achieved great success, partly because of the popularity of the theatre productions that were inspired by the book. These plays, like most of the films that followed, changed and simplified Mary's original *Frankenstein*.

But the book flourished and lasted, and Mary's story eventually became one of creative breakthrough. *Frankenstein* is widely considered to be the first modern novel of science fiction.

Finally, a P.S. — in this case standing for 'Polidori's story'. Byron's doctor also had literary ambitions. He was the only member of the group besides Mary who actually finished and published a story in response to the famous challenge. Inspired by a fragment of Lord Byron's writing, Polidori wrote a story called *The Vampyre*. It wasn't a great story. But its portrayal of a romantic, aristocratic vampire helped to inspire a later, better vampire tale — Bram Stoker's *Dracula*. It's possible, therefore, that the evening that inspired the greatest monster of science fiction may have also helped to inspire the greatest vampire of the horror genre.

No wonder so many readers over the years have been gripped. A dark and stormy night, five bright, young, unconventional minds — and one of the most fascinating stories of literary creativity ever told.

At the centre of it all was Mary Shelley. She was only eighteen, and she wrote *Frankenstein*.